RAGS TO RICHES

A GUIDE TO ACHIEVING FINANCIAL SUCCESS

JOY DANIELS

TABLE OF CONTENT

INTRODUCTION 5

CHAPTER 1: UNVEILING THE MINDSET OF FINANCIAL SUCCESS.................................... 7

-The psychology of wealth..................... 9

- Identifying and overcoming limiting beliefs .. 13

- Cultivating a positive money mindset 17

CHAPTER 2: MASTERING THE ART OF GOAL SETTING.. 22

- Setting realistic and achievable financial goals
.... 25

- Creating a roadmap for success 29

- The power of visualization in manifesting wealth 34

CHAPTER 3: BREAKING FREE FROM THE CHAINS OF DEBT 39

- Strategies for debt elimination...................... 42

- Building a sustainable budget....................... 46

- Leveraging debt wisely for investment 51

CHAPTER 4: INCOME MULTIPLICATION TECHNIQUES 57

- Maximizing earning potential in your current career.. 60

- Additional income streams 65

- The entrepreneurial mindset: starting and scaling a side business 70

CHAPTER 5: THE SCIENCE OF SMART INVESTING 76

- Investment vehicles (stocks, bonds, real estate) 79

- Risk management and diversification............. 85

- Long-term wealth-building strategies............. 90

CONCLUSION 96

INTRODUCTION

Welcome to "From Rags to Riches: A Guide to Achieving Financial Success," an empowering journey through the strategies and mindset shifts that can transform your financial trajectory. In this book, we embark on a compelling exploration of how individuals, regardless of their starting point, can pave their way to prosperity and abundance.

Financial success is a universal aspiration, and many dream of transcending limitations to build wealth from humble beginnings. "From Rags to Riches" is not just a collection of success stories; it's a practical guide infused with actionable insights, proven techniques, and timeless principles that can empower you to take control of your financial destiny.

Drawing from real-world examples, psychological studies, and financial expertise, this book delves into the core principles that underpin success in wealth creation. Whether you're navigating the challenges of debt, aiming to multiply your income, or seeking to invest wisely, the strategies presented here are tailored to meet you where you are on your financial journey.

The journey from rags to riches is not solely about monetary gains; it's about cultivating a mindset that fosters financial intelligence, resilience, and adaptability. We explore the importance of goal-setting, disciplined saving, strategic investing, and the cultivation of a positive relationship with money. Moreover, we address the psychological barriers that often hinder financial progress and offer actionable steps to overcome them.

"From Rags to Riches" is more than a guide; it's a roadmap to financial empowerment. Whether you're a recent graduate, a seasoned professional, or anyone striving for financial security, this book equips you with the tools to turn your dreams into a tangible reality. Get ready to embark on a transformative journey toward lasting financial success!

CHAPTER 1: UNVEILING THE MINDSET OF FINANCIAL SUCCESS

Welcome to the foundational chapter of "From Rags to Riches: A Guide to Achieving Financial Success." In this crucial section, we delve deep into the heart of prosperity—the mindset. Success in the realm of wealth creation is not merely about monetary strategies; it begins with a transformative shift in the way we perceive and interact with money.

This chapter serves as a powerful lens through which we explore the intricate connection between our thoughts, beliefs, and financial outcomes. By unveiling the mindset of financial success, we embark on a journey of self-discovery and awareness, uncovering the psychological patterns that may be hindering our progress.

We start by understanding the psychology of wealth and examining the beliefs and attitudes that shape our financial reality. From ingrained notions about money to societal influences, we peel back the layers to reveal the core mindset principles that underpin lasting success.

Moreover, this chapter goes beyond identification; it provides actionable insights on how to cultivate a positive money mindset. Through practical exercises, real-life anecdotes, and expert guidance, readers will gain the tools needed to reshape their financial worldview. We explore the transformative power of optimism, resilience, and a can-do attitude in the face of financial challenges.

As we journey through "Unveiling the Mindset of Financial Success," prepare to challenge assumptions, embrace a new perspective, and lay the groundwork for a mindset that paves the way to prosperity. The principles uncovered in this chapter will set the stage for the practical strategies and techniques detailed in the subsequent chapters, ensuring that the path to financial success is not only navigable but transformative. Get ready to redefine your relationship with money and unlock the mindset that leads to enduring financial abundance.

-The psychology of wealth

The psychology of wealth encompasses the intricate interplay between an individual's thoughts, emotions, and behaviors related to money. Understanding this psychological aspect is pivotal in the pursuit of financial success. Here are key elements that contribute to the psychology of wealth:

1. **Beliefs and Attitudes:**

  - *Money Scripts:* People develop "money scripts" based on early experiences and upbringing, influencing their beliefs about money. These scripts can be positive or limiting, shaping financial decisions and behaviors.

 - *Attitudes Toward Wealth:* Examining one's attitudes toward wealth and success is crucial. Some may view wealth as a source of security and opportunity, while others may harbour subconscious negative beliefs that hinder financial progress.

2. Money Mindset:

 - *Abundance vs. Scarcity Mindset:* A person's mindset can be categorized as either abundance or scarcity. An abundance mindset focuses on opportunities, collaboration, and growth, while a scarcity mindset fixates on limitations, fear of loss, and competition.

 - *Fixed vs. Growth Mindset:* Drawing from Carol Dweck's work, individuals with a growth mindset see challenges as opportunities to learn and grow, while those with a fixed mindset may avoid challenges to protect their self-image.

3. **Financial Self-Efficacy:**

 - *Confidence in Financial Abilities:* Financial self-efficacy relates to one's confidence in their ability to manage money effectively. Building this confidence involves acquiring financial literacy, setting and achieving financial goals, and overcoming challenges.

4. **Delayed Gratification:**

 - *Time Perspective:* The ability to delay gratification is linked to a person's time perspective. Those who can defer immediate rewards for long-term gain tend to make more prudent financial decisions.

5. **Emotional Influences:**

 - *Emotions and Decision-Making:* Emotional intelligence plays a significant role in financial decisions. Being aware of and managing emotions like fear, greed, and impulsivity is crucial for making rational and beneficial choices.

6. Social and Cultural Factors:

- *Social Comparisons:* People often compare their financial status to others, impacting self-worth and satisfaction. Understanding the psychological effects of social comparisons can help individuals navigate societal pressures and make informed financial choices.

7. Lifestyle Inflation:

- *Adaptation and Satisfaction:* Individuals may experience "lifestyle inflation" as their income increases, adapting their spending habits to match higher earnings. Awareness of this phenomenon can help manage lifestyle choices in alignment with long-term financial goals.

Understanding the psychology of wealth provides a foundation for personal growth and financial success. By recognizing and reshaping limiting beliefs, fostering a positive mindset, and addressing emotional influences, individuals can cultivate a psychological framework that propels them toward enduring prosperity.

- Identifying and overcoming limiting beliefs

Identifying and overcoming limiting beliefs is a crucial step in the journey towards financial success. These beliefs, often ingrained in our subconscious, can act as significant barriers to achieving our full potential. Here's a step-by-step process to help individuals recognize and conquer limiting beliefs:

1. **Self-Reflection:**

   - Begin by reflecting on your beliefs about money. Consider your upbringing, past experiences, and the messages you've received about wealth. Identify any recurring negative thoughts or attitudes that may be hindering your financial progress.

2. Awareness of Negative Patterns:

- Pay attention to your thoughts and behaviors related to money. Recognize patterns of self-sabotage, self-doubt, or avoidance when it comes to financial decisions. Awareness is the first step toward breaking free from limiting beliefs.

3. Questioning Beliefs:

- Challenge your beliefs by asking critical questions. Are these beliefs based on facts or assumptions? Where did they originate? Are they helping or hindering your financial goals? Questioning the validity of limiting beliefs can create space for more empowering perspectives.

4. Seek External Perspectives:

- Talk to mentors, friends, or professionals about your beliefs. External perspectives can provide valuable insights and alternative viewpoints. Others may offer guidance based on their experiences, helping you see your situation from a different angle.

5. **Cognitive Restructuring:**

- Engage in cognitive restructuring, a process of reframing negative thoughts into positive, empowering ones. Replace limiting beliefs with affirmations that align with your financial goals. For example, transform "I'll never be financially secure" into "I am actively working towards financial security."

6. **Education and Skill Development:**

- Sometimes, limiting beliefs stem from a lack of knowledge or skills. Invest time in financial education and skill development to boost your confidence and competence. Acquiring new knowledge can challenge and dispel unfounded beliefs.

7. **Visualization Techniques:**

- Use visualization to imagine a future where your financial goals are achieved. Visualizing success can help reprogram your subconscious mind, making it more receptive to positive beliefs and affirmations.

8. **Gradual Exposure:**

- Gradually expose yourself to situations that challenge your limiting beliefs. Start with small, manageable steps that push your comfort zone. As you experience success in overcoming challenges, your confidence will grow.

9. **Accountability and Support:**

- Share your financial goals and efforts to overcome limiting beliefs with a trusted friend, family member, or mentor. Having someone hold you accountable can provide support and encouragement throughout the process.

10. **Celebrate Progress:**

- Celebrate small victories along the way. Acknowledge and celebrate the positive changes you make in your mindset and financial behavior. Recognizing progress reinforces the belief that change is possible.

Identifying and overcoming limiting beliefs is an ongoing process that requires self-awareness, intentional effort, and a commitment to personal growth. By actively challenging and replacing negative beliefs with empowering ones, individuals can create a mindset conducive to financial success.

- Cultivating a positive money mindset

Cultivating a positive money mindset is a transformative process that involves reshaping your thoughts, attitudes, and beliefs about money. Adopting a positive money mindset can have profound effects on your financial well-being and overall life satisfaction. Here's a step-by-step process to guide you through this journey:

1. **Self-Awareness:**

   - Begin by becoming aware of your current beliefs and attitudes towards money. Identify any negative or limiting thoughts that may be holding you back. Awareness is the first step in bringing about positive change.

2. Challenge Negative Thoughts:

- Actively challenge and reframe negative thoughts about money. When you catch yourself thinking, "I'll never be financially successful," replace it with a positive affirmation like "I am on the path to financial success, and every step forward is a victory."

3. Gratitude Practice:

- Cultivate gratitude for the money you have and the opportunities it provides. Regularly acknowledge and appreciate the financial aspects of your life, whether big or small. Gratitude shifts focus from scarcity to abundance.

4. Focus on Abundance:

- Shift your mindset from scarcity to abundance. Instead of dwelling on what you lack, focus on what you have and the opportunities available to you. Embrace the belief that there is always enough to spare.

5. **Set Positive Financial Goals:**

- Define clear and positive financial goals. Instead of framing goals in terms of avoiding debt or financial stress, set goals that express what you want to achieve, such as building an emergency fund, saving for a dream vacation, or investing for the future.

6. **Educate Yourself:**

- Expand your financial knowledge and literacy. Understanding how money works and learning about personal finance empowers you to make informed and positive financial decisions. Education is a key element in building confidence.

7. **Surround Yourself with Positivity:**

- Surround yourself with positive influences. Engage with people who have a healthy and positive relationship with money. Their mindset and behaviors can inspire and reinforce your efforts to cultivate a positive money mindset.

8. **Practice Mindfulness:**

 - Embrace mindfulness practices to stay present and avoid dwelling on financial worries from the past or anxieties about the future. Mindfulness can help you make conscious and positive financial decisions in the present moment.

9. **Affirmations and Visualization:**

 - Create positive affirmations related to money and repeat them regularly. Visualization techniques can also be powerful; imagine achieving your financial goals and visualize the positive emotions associated with financial success.

10. **Celebrate Financial Wins:**

 - Celebrate your financial achievements, no matter how small. Acknowledge your progress and use it as motivation to continue cultivating a positive money mindset.

11. **Practice Generosity:**

 - Engage in acts of generosity, whether through charitable giving or helping others in your community. Acts of kindness and generosity contribute to a positive money mindset by reinforcing the idea that money can be a force for good.

Cultivating a positive money mindset is an ongoing practice that involves conscious effort and a commitment to personal growth. By embracing positivity, gratitude, and a forward-looking perspective, individuals can create a mindset that attracts financial abundance and success.

CHAPTER 2: MASTERING THE ART OF GOAL SETTING

Welcome to the transformative journey of "Mastering the Art of Goal Setting," the pivotal chapter in "From Rags to Riches: A Guide to Achieving Financial Success." In this section, we delve into the profound impact that strategic goal setting can have on shaping your financial destiny. Beyond mere aspirations, goal setting is the compass that directs your actions, propelling you toward the financial success you envision.

This chapter serves as a roadmap, guiding you through the intricate process of defining, refining, and pursuing financial goals that align with your deepest aspirations. We explore the art of setting goals that not only inspire but also serve as tangible stepping stones on your path from financial struggle to abundance.

Understanding the Power of Goals:

- Discover the intrinsic connection between clarity of purpose and financial success. Uncover how well-defined goals act as catalysts for motivation, focus, and a sense of direction in your financial journey.

Setting Realistic and Achievable Goals:

- Dive into the nuances of setting goals that are both challenging and attainable. Learn to strike the delicate balance between ambition and feasibility, ensuring that your goals ignite passion without becoming sources of overwhelming stress.

Creating a Roadmap for Success:

- Explore the strategic planning process that transforms your goals into a comprehensive roadmap. Understand the importance of breaking down larger objectives into manageable tasks, making your financial journey not only feasible but also enjoyable.

The Power of Visualization in Manifesting Wealth:

- Delve into the psychological influence of visualization on goal attainment. Uncover techniques to vividly imagine and internalize your financial success, harnessing the power of your mind to manifest the reality you desire.

This chapter is not just about setting goals—it's about mastering the art of goal setting. It equips you with the tools to turn your dreams into actionable plans, providing a structured approach to financial success. As we embark on this exploration, be prepared to define your aspirations, refine your strategies, and witness the profound impact that mastering the art of goal setting can have on your journey from rags to riches. Get ready to sculpt the future you desire, one goal at a time.

- Setting realistic and achievable financial goals

Setting realistic and achievable financial goals is a crucial aspect of personal financial planning. Well-defined goals provide a roadmap for your financial journey, helping you stay focused and motivated. Here's a step-by-step process to guide you in setting realistic and achievable financial goals:

1. **Self-Reflection:**

   - Begin by reflecting on your values, priorities, and long-term aspirations. Consider what financial success looks like to you and how it aligns with your overall life goals. This self-awareness forms the foundation for setting meaningful financial goals.

2. **Define Clear Objectives:**

- Clearly articulate your financial objectives. Whether it's building an emergency fund, paying off debt, saving for a home, or investing for retirement, specificity is key. The more precise your goals, the easier it is to develop a targeted plan.

3. **Prioritize Goals:**

- Prioritize your financial goals based on urgency and importance. Distinguish between short-term, medium-term, and long-term goals. This helps you allocate resources effectively and ensures that you're addressing immediate needs while also planning for the future.

4. **Make Goals Measurable:**

- Quantify your goals to make them measurable. For example, instead of a vague goal like "save more money," specify an amount or percentage of your income you intend to save each month. Measurable goals allow you to track progress and celebrate achievements.

5. Set Realistic Timeframes:

- Establish realistic timeframes for achieving each goal. Consider your current financial situation, income, and other commitments. Be mindful of external factors such as economic conditions that may impact your timeline.

6. Consider Affordability:

- Assess the affordability of your goals. Ensure that your financial goals are realistic given your current income, expenses, and obligations. Setting overly ambitious goals that strain your budget can lead to frustration and burnout.

7. Break Down Larger Goals:

- Divide larger, long-term goals into smaller, manageable milestones. Breaking down goals into smaller tasks makes them less overwhelming and allows for incremental progress. It also provides opportunities to celebrate achievements along the way.

8. Align with Income and Resources:

- Ensure that your goals are aligned with your income and available resources. If your goals exceed your current financial capacity, consider adjusting them or exploring ways to increase your income over time.

9. Account for Contingencies:

- Anticipate unexpected challenges or changes in circumstances. Building flexibility into your goal-setting process allows you to adapt to unforeseen events without derailing your entire financial plan.

10. Regularly Review and Adjust:

- Financial goals should be dynamic. Regularly review your progress and reassess your goals as needed. Life circumstances, economic conditions, and personal priorities may change, requiring adjustments to your financial plan.

11. Seek Professional Guidance:

- If needed, consult with financial professionals for guidance. They can provide valuable insights, help refine your goals, and assist in developing a comprehensive financial plan tailored to your unique situation.

Setting realistic and achievable financial goals is a proactive and empowering process. It requires a thoughtful assessment of your values, a clear understanding of your financial situation, and a commitment to incremental progress. By following this process, you can create a roadmap that propels you towards your financial aspirations while ensuring a balanced and sustainable approach to wealth building.

- Creating a roadmap for success

Creating a roadmap for success involves transforming your financial goals into a strategic plan that guides your actions and decisions. This process helps you navigate the journey from where you are to where you want to be. Here's a step-by-step guide to creating a roadmap for financial success:

1. Review and Refine Goals:

- Start by reviewing your financial goals. Ensure they are clear, specific, measurable, and aligned with your values. Refine them as needed based on changes in your circumstances or priorities.

2. Prioritize Goals:

- Prioritize your goals based on their importance and urgency. Identify which goals are short-term, medium-term, and long-term. This hierarchy will guide your focus and resource allocation.

3. Break Down Goals into Tasks:

- Divide each goal into actionable tasks or milestones. Breaking down goals into smaller, manageable steps makes the journey less overwhelming and allows for a more systematic approach.

4. Assign Timeframes:

- Assign realistic timeframes to each task or milestone. Be mindful of deadlines for short-term goals and consider the time required for achieving long-term objectives. This step helps create a timeline for your financial roadmap.

5. Allocate Resources:

- Determine the financial resources required for each task. This includes budgeting for savings, investments, debt repayment, and other expenses related to your goals. Ensure that your financial plan aligns with your income and resources.

6. Create a Budget:

- Develop a comprehensive budget that reflects your income, expenses, and savings goals. A well-structured budget serves as a financial roadmap by providing a clear picture of how your money will be allocated.

7. **Explore Income Opportunities:**

   - Identify opportunities to increase your income, such as exploring additional revenue streams or advancing in your career. A diversified income can enhance your ability to achieve financial goals.

8. **Mitigate Risks:**

   - Anticipate potential risks or obstacles that may arise along the way. Develop contingency plans to mitigate these risks, ensuring that unexpected challenges do not derail your progress.

9. **Implement Tracking Mechanisms:**

   - Set up tracking mechanisms to monitor your progress. This can include financial apps, spreadsheets, or regular check-ins with a financial advisor. Regularly assessing your advancement helps you stay on course and make adjustments as needed.

10. **Celebrate Milestones:**

   - Celebrate achievements and milestones along the way. Acknowledge your progress, no matter how small, and use these celebrations as motivation to continue pursuing your financial roadmap.

11. **Review and Adjust Periodically:**

- Periodically review and adjust your roadmap based on changes in your life, financial situation, or external factors. Flexibility is key to adapting your plan to evolving circumstances.

12. **Seek Professional Guidance:**

- Consider consulting with financial professionals for expert advice. Financial advisors can provide insights, offer tailored strategies, and help optimize your financial roadmap for success.

Creating a roadmap for financial success is an ongoing and dynamic process. It requires careful planning, discipline, and adaptability. By following these steps, you can turn your financial goals into a structured plan that guides your actions, helping you navigate the complexities of wealth-building and achieve lasting financial success.

- The power of visualization in manifesting wealth

The power of visualization in manifesting wealth is a psychological and motivational technique that involves creating vivid mental images of achieving financial success. This practice harnesses the mind's ability to influence behaviors, attitudes, and outcomes. Here's how the power of visualization can impact your journey to wealth:

1. **Clarifying Goals:**

   - Visualization provides a clear picture of your financial goals. By vividly imagining the life you want to lead, including the level of wealth you desire, you create a mental blueprint that guides your actions and decisions.

2. **Activating the Reticular Activating System (RAS):**

- The brain's Reticular Activating System is responsible for filtering information and focusing on what's deemed important. Visualization programs the RAS to be more attuned to opportunities and resources that align with your financial goals, making you more receptive to wealth-building possibilities.

3. **Building Confidence:**

- Visualization cultivates a sense of confidence and self-efficacy. By regularly visualizing success, you reinforce the belief that achieving financial goals is not only possible but also within your capabilities. This increased confidence positively influences your financial behaviors.

4. **Reducing Stress and Anxiety:**

- Visualization helps alleviate financial stress and anxiety by shifting the focus from potential challenges to envisioned success. This mental rehearsal can create a more positive and proactive mindset, reducing the emotional toll of financial concerns.

5. Enhancing Motivation:

- Visualization serves as a powerful motivator. Imagining the benefits of financial success, such as security, freedom, and the ability to pursue meaningful experiences, fuels your drive to work towards those goals with greater enthusiasm and determination.

6. Creating Emotional Connection:

- Visualization evokes emotions associated with achieving your financial goals. By emotionally connecting to your vision of wealth, you reinforce a positive relationship with money and increase your commitment to taking the necessary steps to manifest that vision.

7. Programming Subconscious Mind:

- The subconscious mind plays a significant role in shaping behavior. Visualization communicates your financial goals directly to the subconscious, influencing your thoughts, decisions, and actions on a subconscious level.

8. Improving Decision-Making:

- Visualization helps you simulate various financial scenarios in your mind. This mental rehearsal enhances your ability to make informed and strategic decisions, as you've already visualized potential outcomes and responses.

9. Fostering Creativity and Innovation:

- Visualization stimulates creative thinking by encouraging you to explore innovative ways to achieve your financial goals. This creativity can lead to the discovery of new opportunities and strategies for wealth creation.

10. Consistency in Action:

- Visualization promotes consistency in taking action towards your goals. The mental rehearsal of success can serve as a daily reminder of your objectives, reinforcing your commitment and dedication to the steps necessary for wealth manifestation.

11. Aligning Mind and Behavior:

- Visualization aligns your mental state with your desired behavior. As you consistently visualize success, your actions naturally gravitate towards the behaviors conducive to achieving financial goals.

To effectively harness the power of visualization in manifesting wealth, it's essential to incorporate this practice into your daily routine. Consistency, belief in the process, and a genuine connection to your financial vision will amplify the impact of visualization on your journey to financial success.

CHAPTER 3:
BREAKING FREE FROM THE CHAINS OF DEBT

Welcome to a chapter that holds the promise of liberation — "Breaking Free from the Chains of Debt." In this pivotal section of "From Rags to Riches: A Guide to Achieving Financial Success," we embark on a transformative exploration of strategies and insights to liberate ourselves from the burden of debt, paving the way for true financial freedom.

Debt, like heavy chains, can constrain our ability to realize our dreams and live life on our terms. Yet, within the pages of this chapter, we unravel the means to break these chains and reclaim control over our financial destinies. By understanding the intricacies of debt and implementing practical, actionable solutions, we unlock the potential for a debt-free existence.

Understanding the Weight of Debt:

- We begin by delving into the psychology of debt, exploring the emotional toll it takes and how it can limit our financial potential. Recognizing the impact of debt is the first step towards breaking free.

Strategies for Debt Elimination:

- The heart of this chapter lies in a comprehensive examination of strategies for debt elimination. From the snowball and avalanche methods to negotiating with creditors, we dissect proven approaches that empower individuals to regain control over their financial well-being.

Building a Sustainable Budget:

- A pivotal aspect of breaking free from debt is the cultivation of financial discipline through budgeting. We explore the art of creating a sustainable budget that not only helps manage existing debt but also prevents its recurrence, laying the foundation for lasting financial stability.

Leveraging Debt Wisely for Investment:

- While we advocate for liberation from oppressive debt, we also recognize the potential benefits of leveraging debt strategically for wealth-building. Learn how to distinguish between good and bad debt, and explore how judicious use of credit can propel you towards financial success.

This chapter is not just about escaping the chains of debt; it's about forging a new, empowered relationship with your finances. As we navigate through strategies, stories, and practical guidance, anticipate a transformation — a transformation that liberates you from the weight of debt and sets you on a course towards financial resilience and prosperity. Get ready to break free and embrace a future unburdened by the chains of debt.

- Strategies for debt elimination

Implementing effective strategies for debt elimination is a crucial step in achieving financial freedom and building a secure future. Here are key strategies that individuals can employ to break free from the shackles of debt:

1. **Create a Comprehensive Debt Inventory:**

   - Begin by compiling a detailed list of all your debts. Include information such as the total amount owed, interest rates, and minimum monthly payments. This inventory serves as the foundation for developing a targeted debt elimination plan.

2. **Prioritize Debts:**

   - Prioritize your debts based on interest rates or the "debt snowball" method, where you focus on paying off the smallest debt first while making minimum payments on others. Both approaches have psychological and financial benefits, providing motivation or minimizing interest costs.

3. Negotiate Interest Rates:

- Contact creditors to negotiate lower interest rates. A lower interest rate means more of your payments go towards reducing the principal, accelerating the debt-elimination process.

4. Increase Income:

- Explore opportunities to increase your income, such as taking on a side job or freelancing. Allocating additional income towards debt repayment can expedite the elimination process.

5. Create a Realistic Budget:

- Develop a comprehensive budget that accounts for all your income and expenses. Identify areas where you can cut discretionary spending and allocate those funds towards debt repayment.

6. Use Windfalls Wisely:

- Utilize unexpected windfalls, such as tax refunds or bonuses, to make lump-sum payments towards your debts. This accelerates the reduction of the principal amount owed.

7. Consider Debt Consolidation:

- Explore debt consolidation options to streamline multiple debts into a single, more manageable payment. This can simplify your financial obligations and, in some cases, lower your overall interest rate.

8. Automate Payments:

- Set up automatic payments for minimum amounts on all debts and allocate any additional funds towards the highest-priority debt. Automation ensures consistency and reduces the likelihood of missed payments.

9. Financial Windfall Strategy:

- If you receive a financial windfall, such as an inheritance or settlement, consider using a portion or the entirety of it to eliminate high-interest debts. This can significantly accelerate your journey to debt freedom.

10. Seek Professional Advice:

- Consult with a financial advisor or credit counsellor for personalized guidance. They can help you explore debt management strategies, negotiate with creditors, and provide expert advice tailored to your specific situation.

11. Stay Committed to Lifestyle Changes:

- Cultivate a mindset of financial discipline and commit to long-term lifestyle changes. Avoid accumulating new debt and embrace frugal habits that support your debt-elimination goals.

12. **Emergency Fund Establishment:**

- Simultaneously work on building an emergency fund. Having a financial cushion can prevent the need to rely on credit for unexpected expenses, mitigating the risk of accumulating more debt.

Successful debt elimination requires a combination of financial planning, discipline, and strategic decision-making. Tailoring these strategies to your unique circumstances and staying committed to the process can lead to a debt-free and financially secure future. Remember, the journey to debt freedom is gradual, but each step brings you closer to financial independence.

- Building a sustainable budget

Building a sustainable budget is a fundamental step in achieving financial stability and working towards your financial goals. A sustainable budget balances income and expenses while allowing for savings and debt reduction. Here's a comprehensive guide to help you create and maintain a sustainable budget:

1. Calculate Your Income:

- Determine your total monthly income. Include all sources such as salary, freelance work, rental income, and any other consistent inflows. This provides a clear understanding of the financial resources available for budgeting.

2. List Your Expenses:

- Make a comprehensive list of your monthly expenses. Categorize them into fixed (mortgage/rent, utilities, insurance) and variable (groceries, dining out, entertainment). Account for irregular expenses such as annual subscriptions or maintenance costs.

3. Identify Non-Essential Expenses:

- Examine your variable expenses and identify non-essential items. These are areas where you can potentially cut back or make adjustments. Creating a clear distinction between needs and wants is crucial for budget sustainability.

4. Set Financial Goals:

- Define short-term and long-term financial goals. Whether it's building an emergency fund, paying off debt, or saving for a specific purpose, align your budget with these goals. This ensures that your spending supports your broader financial objectives.

5. Allocate for Savings and Debt Repayment:

- Prioritize savings and debt repayment in your budget. Allocate a specific portion of your income to build an emergency fund and make consistent payments towards any outstanding debts. This helps you avoid accumulating additional debt and fosters financial resilience.

6. Create Budget Categories:

- Organize your budget into categories based on your spending habits and financial priorities. Common categories include housing, transportation, food, utilities, entertainment, and personal care.

Assign specific amounts to each category based on your calculated expenses.

7. **Use the 50/30/20 Rule:**

   - Consider the 50/30/20 rule as a guideline. Allocate 50% of your income to necessities, 30% to discretionary spending, and 20% to savings and debt repayment. Adjustments can be made based on your specific financial goals and circumstances.

8. **Regularly Review and Adjust:**

   - Regularly review your budget to ensure it remains aligned with your financial goals and reflects any changes in your income or expenses. Life circumstances may evolve, and your budget should adapt accordingly.

9. **Emergency Fund:**

   - Include a category for an emergency fund in your budget. This fund serves as a financial safety net, protecting you from unexpected expenses and reducing the likelihood of relying on credit in times of crisis.

10. **Use Budgeting Tools:**

- Leverage budgeting tools and apps to track your income and expenses. These tools can provide real-time insights, facilitate goal tracking, and automate certain aspects of your budget management.

11. **Involve Family Members:**

- If applicable, involve family members in the budgeting process. Ensure that everyone is on board with the financial goals and understands the importance of adhering to the budget. This collective effort enhances the sustainability of the budget.

12. **Celebrate Milestones:**

- Celebrate achievements and milestones in your budgeting journey. Whether it's reaching a savings goal or successfully paying off a debt, acknowledging progress reinforces positive financial habits.

Building a sustainable budget is an ongoing process that requires commitment, adaptability, and a proactive approach to financial management. By following these steps, you can create a budget that not only meets your immediate needs but also positions you for long-term financial success.

- Leveraging debt wisely for investment

Leveraging debt wisely for investment involves using borrowed funds strategically to potentially generate returns that outweigh the cost of the debt. This approach can enhance investment opportunities and wealth-building if executed with careful consideration and risk management. Here's a guide to the process of leveraging debt for investment:

1. **Understand the Difference Between Good and Bad Debt:**

   - Distinguish between good and bad debt. Good debt is used to finance assets that have the potential to appreciate or generate income, such as real estate or investments. Bad debt, on the other hand, typically involves borrowing for non-appreciating assets or consumables.

2. Evaluate Investment Opportunities:

- Conduct thorough research and due diligence on potential investment opportunities. Whether it's real estate, stocks, or a business venture, assess the risk and return profile. The goal is to identify investments with the potential for positive returns that exceed the cost of borrowing.

3. Calculate the Cost of Debt:

- Understand the terms of the debt you're considering, including interest rates, fees, and repayment terms. Calculate the total cost of borrowing to determine whether the potential returns on the investment outweigh the costs associated with the debt.

4. Assess Risk Tolerance:

- Evaluate your risk tolerance. Leveraging debt for investment introduces an element of risk, and it's essential to assess your comfort level with potential fluctuations in the value of your investments and the ability to meet debt obligations.

5. Establish a Clear Investment Plan:

- Develop a clear and well-defined investment plan. Outline your investment objectives, strategies, and exit strategies. Having a structured plan helps guide your decisions and minimizes impulsive actions that may be influenced by market fluctuations.

6. Use Leverage Strategically:

- Use leverage strategically, focusing on investments that have the potential to provide returns that surpass the cost of borrowing. Avoid excessive leverage, as it can amplify both gains and losses.

7. Consider Tax Implications:

- Assess the tax implications of leveraging for investment. In some cases, the interest on investment-related debt may be tax-deductible, enhancing the overall financial benefit.

8. Diversify Investments:

- Diversify your investments to spread risk. Avoid concentrating all leveraged funds into a single investment, as this can expose you to significant risk if that particular asset underperforms.

9. Monitor and Adjust:

- Regularly monitor the performance of your investments and the cost of debt. Be prepared to adjust your strategy based on market conditions, changes in interest rates, or shifts in your financial circumstances.

10. Have an Exit Strategy:

- Establish a clear exit strategy. Knowing when and how you'll liquidate your investments to repay the borrowed funds is crucial. Having a well-defined plan minimizes the risk of financial distress.

11. **Reinvest Returns Wisely:**

- Reinvest returns from leveraged investments strategically. Consider using profits to pay down debt, further invest in appreciating assets, or diversify into other opportunities.

12. **Seek Professional Advice:**

- Consult with financial advisors, investment professionals, or tax experts. Their expertise can provide valuable insights, help you navigate complex financial decisions, and ensure that leveraging debt for investment aligns with your overall financial goals.

Leveraging debt for investment is a sophisticated financial strategy that requires careful planning, research, and risk management. When executed wisely, it has the potential to accelerate wealth-building and enhance financial outcomes. However, it's essential to approach such strategies with caution and seek professional guidance to make informed decisions based on your unique financial situation and goals.

CHAPTER 4: INCOME MULTIPLICATION TECHNIQUES

Welcome to a transformative journey into the realm of financial empowerment — "Income Multiplication Techniques." In this pivotal chapter of "From Rags to Riches: A Guide to Achieving Financial Success," we delve into proven strategies and innovative approaches to amplify your earning potential. As we navigate through the intricacies of income multiplication, the aim is not just financial stability but the realization of your dreams and aspirations.

Your income is the cornerstone of financial well-being, and in this chapter, we unlock the secrets to multiplying it strategically. From exploring diverse income streams to enhancing your earning capacity through skill development, we embark on a comprehensive exploration of techniques designed to propel you towards financial abundance.

Understanding the Dynamics of Income:

- We begin by unravelling the dynamics of income — its sources, limitations, and untapped possibilities. Understanding the landscape of your earning potential is essential for charting a course towards multiplication.

Diversifying Income Streams:

- Explore the concept of diversifying income streams as a means of building resilience and unlocking new avenues for financial growth. We uncover strategies to cultivate multiple streams of income that align with your skills, passions, and the ever-evolving market.

Investing in Skill Development:

- The value of your skills is a direct contributor to your earning capacity. Discover the transformative impact of investing in skill development and continuous learning. Acquiring new competencies not only enhances your marketability but also positions you for lucrative opportunities.

Entrepreneurship and Side Ventures:

- Delve into the world of entrepreneurship and side ventures as powerful instruments for income multiplication. Whether launching a small business, freelancing, or engaging in the gig economy, we explore how these endeavors can be catalysts for financial success.

Passive Income Strategies:

- Uncover the allure of passive income — earnings that require minimal effort to maintain. From investments to royalties and real estate, we explore avenues that allow you to generate income while retaining flexibility and time for other pursuits.

This chapter isn't just about increasing the digits on your paycheck; it's about cultivating a mindset and adopting strategies that open doors to untapped financial potential. As we embark on this exploration, envision a future where your income multiplies, providing not just financial stability but the freedom to live life on your terms. Get ready to unlock the techniques that will elevate your financial journey from mere survival to thriving abundance. Welcome to the world of income multiplication.

- Maximizing earning potential in your current career

Maximizing your earning potential in your current career involves a strategic approach that combines skill development, proactive career management, and effective negotiation. Here's a comprehensive process to help you enhance your earning capacity within your existing career:

1. **Self-Assessment:**

   - Begin by conducting a thorough self-assessment. Identify your strengths, skills, and areas of expertise within your current role. Understand how your contributions align with the goals and objectives of your organization.

2. Set Clear Career Goals:

- Define clear and realistic career goals. Consider both short-term and long-term objectives that align with your professional aspirations. Having a clear vision provides direction for your efforts to maximize your earning potential.

3. Continuous Learning and Skill Development:

- Invest in continuous learning and skill development. Stay abreast of industry trends, acquire new certifications, and enhance your existing skills. Proactively seek opportunities for professional development within your current role.

4. Showcase Your Value:

- Communicate and showcase the value you bring to the organization. Quantify your achievements, highlight your contributions, and demonstrate how your work positively impacts the company's success. A strong track record strengthens your position when negotiating for higher compensation.

5. Network Within the Organization:

- Build strong relationships and networks within your organization. Networking can provide insights into potential advancement opportunities, and positive relationships with key decision-makers may enhance your visibility when it comes to promotions or salary discussions.

6. Take on Additional Responsibilities:

- Volunteer for additional responsibilities or projects that align with your skills and interests. Proactively contributing beyond your job description not only demonstrates initiative but also positions you as a valuable asset within the organization.

7. Stay Informed About Industry Salary Trends:

- Research and stay informed about salary trends in your industry and location. Understanding the market value for your role empowers you to negotiate from an informed standpoint during salary discussions.

8. Regular Performance Reviews:

- Utilize performance reviews as opportunities to discuss your career growth and compensation. Come prepared with a list of your accomplishments, areas of improvement, and your vision for contributing to the organization's success.

9. Negotiate Effectively:

- Develop effective negotiation skills. When discussing compensation, be confident, articulate, and well-prepared. Communicate the value you bring to the organization and support your salary expectations with market research and your performance metrics.

10. Explore Promotion Opportunities:

- Actively explore promotion opportunities within your current organization. Discuss career progression with your supervisor and express your interest in advancing to higher roles. Seek feedback on the skills and experiences needed for promotion.

11. Benchmark Your Salary:

- Regularly benchmark your salary against industry standards and comparable roles. If you find that your compensation is below market rates, use this information to negotiate for a more competitive salary.

12. Seek Mentorship and Guidance:

- Seek mentorship and guidance from experienced professionals within your organization. A mentor can provide valuable insights, career advice, and support in navigating the dynamics of career growth and compensation.

Maximizing your earning potential in your current career requires a proactive and strategic approach. By continuously improving your skills, showcasing your value, networking effectively, and negotiating with confidence, you can position yourself for career advancement and increased compensation within your existing role. Remember, the key is to align your efforts with the goals of your organization while ensuring that your skills and contributions are appropriately recognized and rewarded.

- Additional income streams

Diversifying your income through additional streams is a powerful strategy to enhance financial stability, achieve goals, and build wealth. Here are various avenues for creating additional income streams:

1. **Freelancing and Consulting:**

   - Leverage your skills and expertise to offer freelance services or consultancy. Platforms like Upwork, Fiverr, or networking within your industry can connect you with opportunities to provide services on a project basis.

2. **Side Business or Entrepreneurship:**

   - Explore entrepreneurship by starting a side business. This could be anything from an online store, consulting service, or a small business aligned with your passion and expertise.

3. **Investing:**

   - Invest in various financial instruments such as stocks, bonds, mutual funds, or real estate. Investment income can come from dividends, interest, or capital gains, providing a passive income stream.

4. **Real Estate:**

   - Generate income through real estate investments. This can include rental properties, real estate crowdfunding, or house flipping. Rental income provides a consistent stream, while property appreciation can contribute to long-term wealth.

5. **Dividend Stocks:**

- Invest in dividend-paying stocks. Companies that distribute a portion of their profits as dividends can provide a regular income stream for investors.

6. **Online Courses and Content Creation:**

- Monetize your knowledge and skills by creating and selling online courses, e-books, or digital content. Platforms like Udemy or Teachable allow you to reach a global audience.

7. **Affiliate Marketing:**

- Partner with businesses and promote their products or services through affiliate marketing. Earn commissions on sales generated through your referral links.

8. **Passive Income Streams:**

- Explore truly passive income streams, such as royalties from books, music, or intellectual property. This involves creating assets that continue to generate income without ongoing active involvement.

9. Part-Time Work or Gig Economy:

- Take on part-time work or participate in the gig economy. Platforms like Uber, Lyft, or TaskRabbit offer flexible opportunities to earn extra income.

10. Create an Online Presence:

- Build an online presence through blogging, vlogging, or social media. As your audience grows, you can monetize through ads, sponsorships, or selling products/services.

11. Peer-to-Peer Lending:

- Engage in peer-to-peer lending platforms where you can lend money to individuals or small businesses, earning interest on your loans.

12. Royalties and Licensing:

- If you have creative works, consider licensing or selling the rights to your content. This can include photography, artwork, music, or software.

13. **Stock Photography:**

  - If you're a photographer, contribute to stock photo platforms. Each download or purchase of your photos generates income.

14. **Create an E-commerce Store:**

  - Sell products through an e-commerce store. You can either create and sell your products or use drop shipping to sell products without handling inventory.

15. **Automated Online Businesses:**

  - Explore automated online businesses, such as dropshipping or print-on-demand, where fulfilment and shipping are handled by third parties.

16. **Rental Income from Assets:**

  - Rent out assets such as equipment, tools, or even parking spaces to generate additional income.

17. **Online Surveys and Market Research:**

  - Participate in online surveys or market research studies to earn additional income in your free time.

Diversifying income streams not only provides financial security but also offers the flexibility to pursue your passions and interests. It's crucial to carefully assess each opportunity, align it with your skills and interests, and monitor the performance of your various income streams to ensure sustained success.

- The entrepreneurial mindset: starting and scaling a side business

The entrepreneurial mindset is a unique approach to thinking and problem-solving that fosters innovation, risk-taking, and a proactive attitude toward challenges. When applied to starting and scaling a side business, this mindset becomes a driving force for turning ideas into profitable ventures. Here's a discussion on key aspects of the entrepreneurial mindset in the context of launching and expanding a side business:

1. **Vision and Innovation:**

   - Entrepreneurs possess a visionary outlook. They identify opportunities for innovation, seeking novel solutions to problems. In starting a side business, this mindset involves envisioning a unique value proposition that sets the business apart in the market.

2. **Risk-Taking and Resilience:**

   - A willingness to take calculated risks is a hallmark of the entrepreneurial mindset. Starting a side business often involves stepping outside one's comfort zone. Entrepreneurs understand that setbacks are part of the journey and embrace resilience, learning from failures and adapting their strategies.

3. **Proactivity and Initiative:**

   - Entrepreneurs are proactive, seizing opportunities and taking initiative. In the context of a side business, this involves actively pursuing ideas, setting goals, and initiating the necessary steps to bring the business to life.

4. Resourcefulness and Creativity:

- Entrepreneurs exhibit resourcefulness and creativity in problem-solving. When launching a side business, this mindset is reflected in finding innovative ways to leverage existing resources, whether it's time, skills, or limited capital.

5. Customer-Centric Approach:

- Successful entrepreneurs prioritize the needs of their customers. In starting a side business, understanding the target audience, and their pain points, and delivering value is central to building a customer-centric venture.

6. Adaptability and Flexibility:

- The business landscape is dynamic, and entrepreneurs excel at adapting to change. In the context of a side business, being open to feedback, adjusting strategies, and pivoting based on market dynamics are key elements of the entrepreneurial mindset.

7. Goal-Oriented and Strategic Thinking:

- Entrepreneurs set clear goals and develop strategic plans to achieve them. When starting and scaling a side business, this involves creating a roadmap, setting milestones, and continually evaluating progress toward long-term objectives.

8. Networking and Relationship Building:

- Entrepreneurs understand the value of relationships. Building a network of mentors, collaborators, and customers is crucial when starting a side business. Networking provides valuable insights, support, and potential partnerships.

9. Time Management and Productivity:

- Entrepreneurs are adept at managing their time efficiently. When running a side business alongside other commitments, effective time management and productivity become essential for balancing responsibilities.

10. **Financial Literacy and Resource Allocation:**

- Entrepreneurs possess financial acumen. In the context of a side business, this means understanding budgeting, managing cash flow, and making informed decisions about resource allocation.

11. **Continuous Learning and Adaptation:**

- The entrepreneurial mindset thrives on continuous learning. In the realm of a side business, this involves staying informed about industry trends, and new technologies, and adapting to evolving market demands.

12. **Scale-Up Mentality:**

- Entrepreneurs have a scale-up mentality, always seeking ways to expand and grow their ventures. In the context of a side business, this involves identifying opportunities for scalability and planning for sustainable growth.

Cultivating the entrepreneurial mindset when starting and scaling a side business empowers individuals to navigate challenges, seize opportunities, and build ventures that align with their goals and aspirations. It's not just about the business itself but about fostering a mindset that propels personal and professional growth.

CHAPTER 5: THE SCIENCE OF SMART INVESTING

Welcome to a chapter that demystifies the art of investing and brings it into the realm of science — "The Science of Smart Investing." In this pivotal section of "From Rags to Riches: A Guide to Achieving Financial Success," we embark on a journey to unravel the principles, strategies, and methodologies that form the foundation of intelligent and informed investment decisions.

Investing, often perceived as a complex and mysterious endeavor, is indeed a science with its own set of rules, patterns, and data-driven approaches. As we delve into this chapter, we aim to empower you with the knowledge and insights that will elevate your investment acumen from novice to savvy practitioner.

Understanding Market Dynamics:

- We commence by deciphering the intricate dynamics of financial markets. From the forces that drive stock prices to the impact of economic indicators, we unveil the science behind market movements and trends.

Risk Management Strategies:

The science of smart investing places a paramount emphasis on managing risks. We explore proven strategies for risk mitigation, portfolio diversification, and the art of balancing potential returns with prudent risk tolerance.

Data-Driven Decision Making:

- In the age of information, data has become a powerful ally in the world of investments. We dissect the significance of data-driven decision-making, utilizing analytics, financial ratios, and market indicators to inform your investment choices.

Long-Term Wealth Creation:

- The true science of investing extends beyond short-term gains to focus on the principles of long-term wealth creation. We discuss the compounding effect, strategic asset allocation, and other techniques that lay the groundwork for enduring financial success.

Investment Vehicles and Strategies:

- Navigate the landscape of investment vehicles and strategies with confidence. Whether it's understanding the intricacies of stocks, bonds, and mutual funds, or exploring advanced strategies like value investing or dollar-cost averaging, we break down the science behind each option.

This chapter is not just about picking stocks or timing the market; it's about instilling in you a scientific approach to investment decisions. As we unveil the principles of smart investing, anticipate gaining the tools and knowledge to navigate the markets with confidence, make informed choices, and cultivate a portfolio that aligns with your financial objectives. Welcome to the realm where investing transforms from an art into the science of wealth creation.

- Investment vehicles (stocks, bonds, real estate)

Investment vehicles are various instruments or assets that individuals and institutional investors use to allocate their funds with the expectation of generating returns. Each investment vehicle comes with its own risk and return characteristics, making it crucial for investors to understand the nature of these assets. Here's a discussion on three major investment vehicles: stocks, bonds, and real estate.

1. **Stocks:**

Nature:

   - Stocks represent ownership in a company. When investors buy shares of stock, they become partial owners of the company and are entitled to a portion of its profits (dividends) and voting rights in major decisions.

Return Potential:

- Stocks have the potential for high returns, but they are also associated with higher volatility and risk. Stock prices can fluctuate based on company performance, market conditions, and economic factors.

Risk:

- Stocks are considered riskier than some other investment vehicles, especially in the short term. However, over the long term, they have historically provided higher returns compared to many other assets.

Liquidity:

- Stocks are highly liquid, meaning they can be bought or sold quickly in the market. This liquidity provides flexibility for investors to react to market changes.

Diversification:

- Investors can achieve diversification by holding a portfolio of different stocks across industries and sectors. Diversification helps spread risk and mitigate the impact of poor performance in a single stock.

2. Bonds:

Nature:

- Bonds are debt instruments issued by governments, municipalities, or corporations to raise capital. When an investor buys a bond, they are essentially lending money to the issuer in exchange for periodic interest payments and the return of the principal amount at maturity.

Return Potential:

- Bonds typically offer lower returns compared to stocks, but they are considered more stable. The return is determined by the interest rate (coupon) paid by the bond issuer.

Risk:

- Bonds are generally considered lower risk than stocks, especially government bonds. However, there is still the risk of default, particularly with corporate bonds or bonds from financially unstable governments.

Liquidity:

- Bonds are generally less liquid than stocks, and selling them before maturity can result in capital gains or losses. However, the bond market is still relatively liquid compared to some other investments.

Diversification:

- Investors can diversify their bond holdings by investing in different types of bonds, such as government bonds, corporate bonds, or municipal bonds, as well as bonds with varying maturities.

3. Real Estate:

- Real estate involves investing in physical properties, such as residential or commercial properties, land, or real estate investment trusts (REITs). Real estate can generate income through rent and appreciate over time.

Return Potential:

- Real estate offers a potential for both income (rental yield) and capital appreciation. Property values can increase over time, providing a source of wealth.

Risk:

- Real estate is subject to market fluctuations and economic conditions. Additionally, property management and market demand can impact the income generated from rental properties.

Liquidity:

- Real estate is generally less liquid than stocks or bonds. Buying or selling property can take time, and the transaction costs can be significant.

Diversification:

- Investors can diversify their real estate holdings by investing in different types of properties or geographical locations. Real estate investment trusts (REITs) provide a way to invest in a diversified portfolio of real estate assets.

Considerations for Investors:

- The right mix of investment vehicles depends on factors such as the investor's risk tolerance, investment goals, and time horizon. A well-diversified portfolio often includes a combination of stocks, bonds, and real estate to balance risk and return.

Understanding the nature, risks, and potential returns of different investment vehicles is essential for constructing a well-balanced and diversified investment portfolio. Investors should carefully assess their financial goals, risk tolerance, and time horizon before allocating funds to specific investment vehicles.

- Risk management and diversification

Risk management and diversification are fundamental principles in investment strategy, designed to mitigate the impact of potential losses and enhance the overall stability of a portfolio. Here's a discussion of these crucial concepts:

1. **Risk Management:**

Definition:

- Risk management involves identifying, assessing, and mitigating potential risks associated with an investment or a portfolio. It aims to minimize the impact of adverse events on financial goals and protect capital.

Key Aspects of Risk Management:

- **Risk Identification:** Recognizing the various types of risks, including market risk, credit risk, liquidity risk, and operational risk, among others.

- **Risk Assessment:** Evaluating the likelihood and potential impact of identified risks on the investment portfolio.

- **Risk Mitigation:** Implementing strategies to reduce or control risks. This may include diversification, setting stop-loss orders, or using hedging instruments.

Risk Management Strategies:

- **Diversification:** Spreading investments across different asset classes, industries, and geographic regions to reduce concentration risk.

- **Asset Allocation:** Allocating assets based on risk tolerance and investment goals. This involves determining the right mix of stocks, bonds, and other asset classes.

- **Stop-Loss Orders:** Setting predetermined price levels at which to sell an investment to limit potential losses.

- **Derivatives and Hedging:** Using financial instruments like options or futures to hedge against potential losses in the portfolio.

2. Diversification:

Definition:

- Diversification is the practice of spreading investments across a variety of assets to reduce the impact of a poor-performing investment on the overall portfolio. The goal is to achieve a balance between risk and return.

Key Aspects of Diversification:

- **Asset Diversification:** Investing in different types of assets, such as stocks, bonds, real estate, and commodities.

- **Geographic Diversification:** Spreading investments across various geographic regions to minimize the impact of regional economic downturns.

- **Sector Diversification:** Allocating investments across different industry sectors to reduce exposure to sector-specific risks.

- **Company Diversification:** Avoiding concentration in a few individual stocks by investing in a broad range of companies.

Benefits of Diversification:

- **Risk Reduction:** Diversification helps reduce the impact of poor performance in any single investment or asset class.

- **Stability:** A diversified portfolio tends to be more stable over time, as different assets may respond differently to market conditions.

- **Opportunity for Growth:** While diversification aims to minimize risk, it also allows investors to participate in the potential growth of various assets or sectors.

Considerations for Investors:

- **Risk Tolerance:** Investors should assess their risk tolerance, which is the level of uncertainty or potential loss they can comfortably handle. Risk tolerance guides the selection of risk management and diversification strategies.

- **Investment Goals:** The investment goals and time horizon of an investor influence the degree of risk they can afford to take. Longer-term goals may allow for a more aggressive approach, while short-term goals may require a more conservative strategy.

- **Regular Monitoring:** Continuous monitoring of the investment portfolio is essential. As market conditions and economic factors change, adjustments to the portfolio may be necessary to maintain effective risk management and diversification.

In conclusion, effective risk management and diversification are cornerstones of a sound investment strategy. By systematically identifying and mitigating risks and by spreading investments across various assets, investors can build resilient portfolios that are better positioned to weather market fluctuations and pursue long-term financial objectives.

- Long-term wealth-building strategies

Long-term wealth-building strategies involve systematic planning, disciplined execution, and a focus on accumulating assets over an extended period. Successful wealth-building requires a combination of saving, investing, and prudent financial management. Here are key components and strategies for building wealth over the long term:

1. **Setting Clear Financial Goals:**

   - Define clear and realistic financial goals. Whether it's homeownership, retirement, education, or starting a business, having specific objectives provides direction for your wealth-building efforts.

2. Creating a Budget and Saving Consistently:

- Establish a comprehensive budget that outlines income, expenses, and savings goals. Consistent saving, even if it starts with small amounts, is a foundational step in wealth-building.

3. Emergency Fund:

- Build and maintain an emergency fund. This fund serves as a financial safety net, covering unforeseen expenses and preventing the need to dip into long-term investments during emergencies.

4. Debt Management:

- Prioritize debt repayment to reduce interest costs and free up more funds for saving and investing. Focus on high-interest debts first and consider refinancing options.

5. Investing for the Long Term:

- Invest in a diversified portfolio of assets, such as stocks, bonds, and real estate, with a focus on the long term. Taking advantage of compounding returns over time can significantly grow wealth.

6. Retirement Planning:

- Contribute regularly to retirement accounts like 401(k)s or IRAs. Maximize employer contributions and take advantage of tax-advantaged retirement savings options. A long-term focus on retirement planning ensures financial security in later years.

7. Educating Yourself About Investments:

- Stay informed about investment options, market trends, and financial instruments. Educating yourself empowers you to make informed decisions and adapt your investment strategy over the long term.

8. Tax Planning:

- Strategically plan for taxes to minimize liabilities and maximize returns. Utilize tax-advantaged accounts and seek professional advice for tax-efficient investment strategies.

9. Real Estate Investment:

- Consider real estate as a long-term investment. Owning property can provide both rental income and potential appreciation over time, contributing to overall wealth accumulation.

10. Continuing Education and Skill Development:

- Invest in your skills and education to enhance your earning potential. Continuous learning and skill development position you for career growth, salary increases, and entrepreneurial opportunities.

11. Asset Protection:

- Safeguard your wealth by implementing strategies for asset protection. This may include insurance coverage, estate planning, and legal structures to shield assets from unforeseen risks.

12. Automating Savings and Investments:

- Automate your savings and investment contributions. Setting up automatic transfers ensures consistency and discipline in building wealth over the long term.

13. Regular Portfolio Review:

- Periodically review and rebalance your investment portfolio. As financial goals and market conditions change, adjustments may be necessary to align your portfolio with your objectives.

14. Avoiding Short-Term Impulses:

- Resist the temptation to make impulsive financial decisions based on short-term market fluctuations or economic conditions. Stay focused on your long-term goals and avoid reactionary moves.

15. Seeking Professional Guidance:

- Consider seeking advice from financial professionals, such as financial advisors, tax experts, or estate planners. Professional guidance can provide valuable insights and help optimize your wealth-building strategy.

Long-term wealth-building is a gradual process that requires patience, discipline, and a commitment to financial planning. By incorporating these strategies into your financial journey, you can cultivate a solid foundation for building and preserving wealth throughout your life.

CONCLUSION

As we conclude this transformative guide, "Rags to Riches: A Guide to Achieving Financial Success," reflect on the journey we've embarked upon together. From the humble beginnings of financial uncertainty to the empowering principles that pave the way for enduring prosperity, this book has been a roadmap for those aspiring to rewrite their financial narrative.

The stories of individuals who turned adversity into opportunity, coupled with practical strategies and time-tested principles, have illuminated the path to financial success. The journey from rags to riches is not just about accumulating wealth; it's a profound transformation that encompasses mindset, habits, and the relentless pursuit of one's goals.

We've explored the science behind smart investing, the art of income multiplication, the psychology of wealth, and the importance of disciplined financial management. Through the chapters on debt elimination, goal setting, and the power of visualization, you've gained insights that transcend the realm of finances, touching the very essence of personal growth and fulfilment.

As you stand at the intersection of your past struggles and the promise of a prosperous future, remember that this book is not merely a collection of words on pages. It's a guidebook, a companion on your journey, offering practical tools and profound wisdom to navigate the complexities of the financial landscape.

The essence of this guide is captured in the belief that anyone, regardless of their starting point, can shape their financial destiny. It's about making informed choices, cultivating resilience in the face of challenges, and envisioning a future where abundance is not just a destination but a way of life.

In the chapters on risk management and diversification, you've learned to navigate the unpredictable seas of the financial world with skill and prudence. The strategies for long-term wealth-building have laid the groundwork for a future characterized not just by affluence, but by financial freedom, security, and the ability to make a meaningful impact.

As you close this book, carry with you the lessons learned, the dreams rekindled, and the confidence to embark on a journey of sustained financial success. Remember that wealth is not only measured in monetary terms but in the quality of life, you create for yourself and those around you.

May the principles outlined in "Rags to Riches" serve as a guiding light, empowering you to craft a future that transcends the limitations of the past. Your journey to financial success is a story waiting to be written, and with the knowledge gained from these pages, you possess the pen to script a narrative of lasting prosperity.

Here's to your financial success and the wealth of possibilities that lie ahead. May your journey from rags to riches be not just a story but a legacy of resilience, growth, and triumphant achievement?

www.ingramcontent.com/pod-product-compliance
Lightning Source LLC
Chambersburg PA
CBHW070139260726
48658CB00001B/485